Reformed Theology and the Style of Evangelism

Reformed Theology and the Style of Evangelism

John H. Leith

WIPF & STOCK · Eugene, Oregon

REFORMED THEOLOGY AND THE STYLE OF EVANGELISM

Wipf & Stock
An Imprint of Wipf and Stock Publishers
199 W. 8th Ave., Suite 3
Eugene, OR 97401
www.wipfandstock.com

ISBN 13: 978-1-1-60899-702-2

Manufactured in the U.S.A.

"Reformed Theology and the Style of Evangelism" was first published by the Presbyterian Church in the United States, Office of Evangelism and Church Development, in 1973. It was republished by Union Theological Seminary in Virginia circa 1989. It was included in *Pilgrimage of a Presbyterian: Collected Shorter Writings*, edited by Charles E. Raynal (Louisville, Kentucky: Geneva Press, 2001), pp. 288–300.

Foreword

DR. JOHN H. Leith (1919–2002) was the Mary Elizabeth Pemberton Professor of Theology at Union Theological Seminary in Virginia, where he served the church as a theologian and teacher from 1959 until his retirement in 1990. He held degrees from Erskine College, Columbia Theological Seminary, Vanderbilt University, and Yale University. Before joining the Union Theological Seminary faculty, he held pastorates at Second Presbyterian Church in Nashville, Tennessee, and First Presbyterian Church in Auburn, Alabama. He served as moderator for the Synod of North Carolina in 1977–78, and participated on numerous committees of the General Assembly over the years. Beginning in 1984 he served as a member of the PC(USA) Committee to Write a Brief Statement of Faith.

As a pastor and seminary professor, Dr. Leith sustained an interest in Reformed evangelism. He wrote extensively for the church, and his books include: *Creeds of the Church: A Reader in Christian Doctrine, from the Bible to the Present* (1963, 1973, 1982); *The Church: A Believing Fellowship* (1965, 1981); *Assembly at Westminster: Reformed Theology in the Making* (1973, 2008); *An Introduction to the Reformed Tradition: A Way of Being the Christian Community* (1977, 1978, 1981); *The Reformed Imperative: What the Church Has to Say That No One Else Can Say* (1988); *John Calvin's Doctrine of the Christian Life* (1949, 1989, 2010); *From Generation to Generation: The Renewal of the Church According to Its Own Faith and Practice* (1990); *Basic Christian Doctrine* (1993); *Crisis in the Church: The Plight of Theological Education* (1997); and *Pilgrimage of a Presbyterian: Collected Shorter Writings* (2001).

The Foundation for Reformed Theology, which Dr. Leith began, is grateful for the opportunity to keep his works in print and to try to carry on his work in and for the church.

James C. Goodloe IV, Executive Director
Foundation for Reformed Theology

Reformed Theology and the Style of Evangelism

THE RESPONSIBILITY to bear witness to the gracious presence of God in Jesus Christ "in Jerusalem and in all Judea and Samaria and to the end of the earth" has been the perennial task of the Christian community from the beginning. But the style and form of evangelism has varied according to time and place. There is no one way of evangelism, as the history of Christians witnessing and confessing their faith makes very clear. The life of the Christian community has been and is enriched by a variety of evangelistic styles and by multiple theological confessions.

There is, however, a limit to possible Christian theologies, and the preeminent theological task of the church is to test its proclamation by the word of God in Jesus Christ, as attested in scripture, to see that it is within the boundary. There is also a limit to the legitimate styles of evangelism. Some styles of evangelism corrupt and others strengthen the witness, but more significantly, style always betrays the real content. "There is an intimate but seldom seen connection between a person's thought and his style, which Alfred North Whitehead defined precisely as the 'ultimate morality of mind.'"[1]

The purpose of this paper is to relate Reformed theology to the form and style of evangelism. The paper presupposes that evangelism as shaped by Reformed theology is a valid and effective form of evangelism, but it does not presuppose that such form of evangelism is the only form that has validity or effectiveness. It is hoped that the proposal will be the occasion for self-criticism in the work of evangelism and for renewal of theological and ecclesiastical life in the Reformed tradition.

1. Hazelton, *New Accents*, 20.

REFORMED THEOLOGY AND THE STYLE OF EVANGELISM

I

Reformed theology has never been precisely defined, and its boundaries are uncertain. There is no one normative Reformed theology. Here the term is taken in a general sense to indicate the theological perspective that had its origin with Zwingli, Bullinger, and Calvin in sixteenth-century Switzerland and that has been maintained by such theologians as William Ames and Turretin in the seventeenth century, by Edwards in the eighteenth, by Hodge in the nineteenth, and by Karl Barth and Emil Brunner in the twentieth. In order to sharpen its focus, this paper is based specifically on the theological works of Calvin. The most distinguishing characteristics and emphases of classic Reformed theology as embodied in the theology of Calvin were:

1. The lordship and sovereignty of God,
2. History as the working out of the purposes of God,
3. Simplicity in style,
4. The importance of theological knowledge and understanding,
5. The Christian life as the embodiment of the purposes of God and conformity to his will, and
6. The importance of church organization.

Each of these emphases influences the form and shape of evangelism.

The Lordship of God. For Calvin the most important fact is God, and the most important task is the honor and service of God. This is the important truth that older churchmen tried to convey in that strange question alleged to have been put to candidates for the ministry: Are you willing to be damned for the glory of God? However one may judge the merits of the question, it clearly indicated that something is more important than the salvation of one's soul. The question exposed the self-centeredness of those whose own righteousness is too precious and who are excessively concerned with the salvation of their souls. The question also suggests there is something good about the cautious piety of those who seek to do God's will and leave the salvation of their souls to him.

Karl Barth, the great Reformed theologian of the twentieth century, comments that in the theology of Tholuck, a German revival theologian of the nineteenth century, "the religious individual cannot be more important, all the rest cannot be more shapeless, biography cannot replace theology more emphatically, the Christian cause cannot be more thoroughly taken up into the person of the Christian man."[2] For this reason, Barth goes on to say, revival theology can never be great theology. It is too absorbed with the state of the human soul and too little involved with the great reality of God. Revival theology is too eager to report the anatomy of feeling—or the state of the soul—to be able to proclaim adequately the might act of God.

The New Testament scholar, E. C. Colwell, recently observed that in the New Testament,

> We have so little from Jesus about Jesus. He lost Himself in devotion to God. Long before his execution on the cross, he lost his life. Thus be became—to our bafflement—an incarnation of the saying "He who would save his life must lose it."
>
> He talked about our obligation to love God, not about God's love for us. The First Commandment is the central focus of his teaching. And because he had integrity, he talked about that and the second, derivative commandment and not about himself. Love of God came first; love of neighbor followed.
>
> Because of the consistency of this priority in his message, it is difficult to cast his mantle over the current exhortation to find yourself first. The pagan Greeks had a word for it (*Gnothi seauton*), but the good news of Jesus Christ does not. The Gnostics rejoiced in finding themselves, but the majority of Christians would have none of it as the prime quest. For them, as for their Lord, the primal quest was to find God.[3]

2. Barth, *Protestant Theology*, 511.
3. Colwell, *New or Old?*, 105.

Evangelism can never be primarily a means of personal identity or even of personal salvation. It is first of all the acknowledgment of God's gracious presence and loyalty to his cause.

Calvinism also has been characterized by a passionate conviction that purposes of God are being worked out in history. Predestination, writes Eustace Percy in his biography of John Knox, refers not so much to the ultimate destinies of heaven and hell, but to human life in history.[4] The elect person has been called to fulfill the purposes of God in time and space. For this reason the Calvinists became the great converters of culture and transformers of civilization. Christopher Dawson, the Roman Catholic historian of culture, declares that no Christian community has ever exceeded the Calvinists in their understanding of the cultural and historical role of the Christian.[5] Wherever they went they carried with them the vision of holy community, and they sought to transform society into the Christian community.

The holy community was never fully realized in Geneva or Scotland or seventeenth-century Massachusetts. The result was despair. In the context of disappointed hopes, Calvinists were tempted to think of the Christian life as a lonely pilgrimage through this vale of tears and to replace vision of the Christian commonwealth with personal evangelism, conceived as snatching lost souls from the burning.

Another temptation was to define the Christian life exclusively in terms of personal piety instead of responsibility for society. Reformed theology has always been concerned with personal piety, with evangelism as the salvation of the individual soul, and with eternal life as the fulfillment of human existence. But Reformed theology can never be satisfied with the definition of the Christian life simply in these terms. In fact, the abstraction of these dimensions of the Christian life from the fully orbed understanding of salvation that Reformed theology once knew makes

4. Percy, *Knox*, 108ff.

5. Dawson, *Judgment*, 44ff.

their integration back into Reformed theology difficult. Once we define the Christian life as personal piety—as personal evangelism and the salvation of the individual soul—understanding that this is not classical Reformed theology is very difficult. By the same token, the more recent definition of the Christian life simply in terms of social responsibility, of evangelism as social action, and of Christian life as authentic existence in the world also makes it difficult to recover the full dimensions of Christian existence as Reformed theology has understood it.

A third characteristic of Reformed theology is simplicity. Over and over again in liturgy, in lifestyle, in theological writing, Calvin insisted on simplicity. Calvin's intention was never to use two words when one word would do. He did not gild the lily. He disliked embellishment and ornateness. A sermon, a person, a building should be able to communicate who and what they are without ostentation. Simplicity for Calvin was a synonym for integrity. Reality must not be obscured by words, clothing, craftiness, or pompousness of any sort.

Closely related to this emphasis on integrity and simplicity is Calvin's rejection of magic in religion. Magic is on the one hand man's effort to master and control God by fastening the infinite and indeterminate to the finite and determinate. If God, who is creator of heaven and earth, can in some way be tied to what man can control in sacrament, liturgy, or evangelistic procedure, then God himself can be controlled and manipulated. The control of God was the province of the ancient medicine man with his strange ways. This was also the temptation of medieval Catholicism in development of the sacramental system. And it is the peril of some contemporary forms of evangelism as the movie *Marjoe* illustrates.

The human counterpoint of magic as the attempt to manipulate and control God is magic as the endeavor to manipulate human beings and to bypass conscious, responsible decision. Modern psychology has made us aware of the significance of nonverbal communication and of the influence of many forces on personal life that are outside the range of personal awareness. Yet before the days of modern psychology, Luther and Calvin insisted that faith—a responsible, personal decision—was essential to participation in the sacraments. Today the possibility of bypassing conscious personal decision through personal charisma, oratory, or sacraments has been greatly enhanced by the skills of modern psychology and the techniques of modern communication, including mass media. The old Protestant slogan, "No sacrament without faith," must be enlarged to include no evangelism without responsible, conscious, personal decision.

Evangelism in the Reformed tradition can only be conceived in simple, direct, and unadorned fashion. The baroque, or any attempt to overwhelm, is off-limits. The rhetoric of Reformed evangelism will be primarily its content, not the medium of its expression. The medium will express, not obscure, the content. It will seek to convince, not to beguile. Above all, it will be honest and authentic. Reformed evangelism will always be self-critical, subjecting its content and method to continual examination. Only in this way can the evangelist guard against becoming the charlatan. All who have seen the movie *Marjoe* know how effective charlatanry can be and how imperative self-criticism is for those who in any sense speak for God.

A fourth characteristic of the Reformed theology has been an emphasis on knowledge and understanding. Catechetical instruction was one of the primary means of evangelism in Geneva, and admission to the Lord's Table was based on a commitment of life and knowledge of the faith. While Calvin insisted that the knowledge of faith is existential—more of the heart than of the head—he never trusted emotion or feeling when not subjected to critical reflection and rational understanding. While he rejected curiosity and speculation in theology, he clearly stands in the tradition of those who insist that faith seeks understanding. He knew that any religion that requires the sacrifice of the integrity of the human mind with its critical functions is bad religion, for God is the creator of the human mind.

Calvin was an intellectual, believing that all truth comes from God and that the life of the mind may be an important service to God. As a humanist, he did not disdain rational procedure and disciplined study. He did not reject intuition or the significance of direct experience as avenues to truth, but he insisted that disciplined intelligence and direct experience should never be separated. For that reason, he emphasized that Christians should know intellectually as well as personally what they believed.

One of the primary forms that evangelism took in Calvin's Geneva was teaching. The catechetical class was the condition for admission to the Lord's Table. The sacraments were to be administered only in the context of teaching. Preaching in Geneva was instruction in scripture, theology, and Christian living. Indeed, the *Institutes of the Christian Religion* were written as a guide for Bible study and for an intellectual grasp of Christian faith. Calvin regarded the founding of an educational system in Geneva as one of his greatest accomplishments. For Calvin, learning and piety were always joined together.

Evangelism that is rooted in the Reformed tradition must be in large measure teaching. This does not mean that all teaching even in the church is evangelism. Teaching may be and sometimes is heretical in that it does not build up the life of the Christian community. Certainly Calvin knew this. He also knew and believed that there is no evangelism that is not teaching.

A fifth characteristic of Reformed theology is a strong emphasis on the Christian life. The human focus of the Christian life was not self-understanding or the state of the soul or even the vision of God, but a life that embodied the purposes of God. Christian faith was a way of living, deciding, and acting in the world. The Christian person was the responsible person.

Martin Luther had said that the primary use of the law is to convince people that they are sinners and thus to turn them to Christ. In fact, Luther so emphasized the spontaneity of the Christian life that on occasion he could say that Christians no more need the law to tell them how to obey God than a husband needs a law to tell him how to love his wife. Calvin, however, insisted that the primary purpose of the law is to guide and stimulate the Christian in living the good life. He refused to separate law and gospel, as Luther had done. Even in the liturgy of the church he included the Ten Commandments after the prayer of confession and the comfortable words promising forgiveness.

Calvin's emphasis on the law and on ethics led to unfortunate excesses of legalism when the Christian life was defined too exclusively in terms of law, to self-righteousness when Calvinists prematurely convinced themselves that they obeyed the law, and to obscurantism when they uncritically identified the law with a particular pattern of life. The failures of Reformed theology and the consequent caricatures of it should not obscure the real greatness of Calvin's vision of the Christian and the Christian society as embodiments of the purpose of God and of the achievements of that vision in history. No Christians have ever exceeded the Calvinists as shapers of culture and transformers of society.

Evangelism in the Reformed tradition must be concerned with sanctification and must never forget that the gospel includes the law. The call of the evangelist is not simply to an ultimate destiny, but to a way of life here and now in time and space.

II

The sixth distinctive characteristic of Reformed theology is its concern with the organized life of the church. Calvin devoted more than one-fourth of the *Institutes of the Christian Religion* to the "external means of grace." One of his most influential books, probably most influential next to the *Institutes*, was his *Ecclesiastical Ordinances* for the Genevan church. Private Christianity was no more a possibility for Calvin than it was for the New Testament.

To be a Christian is to be the church. Baptism is incorporation into the life of the church. Evangelism is the means by which human beings are related vertically to the God and Father of our Lord Jesus Christ and by which they are horizontally integrated into the one, holy, catholic, and apostolic church.

Evangelism in Reformed theology is always an activity of the church, though not necessarily of the church bureaucracy. It is never the work of a lone-star ranger snatching solitary individuals from the pit and turning them to heaven. Evangelism on the horizontal level is the work of people who are the church, inviting other people to share in the common life of the body of Christ.

Evangelism is incorporation into the community where the word of God is preached and heard and where the sacraments are offered and received. The simplest definition of the church is the community that hears the word of God in faith and obeys in love, for the sacraments are the gospel acted out. There are many different kinds of communities, but the church differs from other communities in that its members share in a common life that is rooted in the word of God. The church is not an aggregation of believers but a communion that shares in common hopes, commitments, and lifestyles, common loves, and common actions.

The common life that is the church is no simple achievement. It cannot be programmed, summoned, or coerced. It is not always evident to human experience. In part, the Christian life is believing that the church exists, as the Apostles' Creed declares, when the reality is not so apparent. Yet the reality does exist, and to this common life, evangelism calls a person on the horizontal level. The dilemma of the evangelists is that they cannot guarantee the church, for the church, like salvation itself, is always the gracious gift of God. As Calvin put it, the church is the elect. The church is the work of the Holy Spirit and the work of Christian people, but it first of all is the work of God's free and sovereign Spirit.

Evangelism is incorporation into a community in which the members are members one of another and share with each other their gifts. One of the signs of the church is the common meal in which bread is shared. The importance of sharing bread cannot be minimized in a world that has such great extremes of wealth. But neither can other signs of the church as the communion of saints be minimized, as for example when the congregation gathers in the face of death to affirm faith that is greater than death, to affirm the reality of the church as a community against a threat to community, and to give real help to fellow members who have been bereaved of the physical presence of a loved one. In our new, secular, pluralistic society, in which many of the traditional props that have supported people in crisis situations are gone, the church is a community that gives support to people as they share in the common life of the body of Christ.

Evangelism is incorporation into a community of theological discourse. Every person is a theologian by the sheer fact of humanity. Human existence is existence filled with decisions. Animals so far as we know do not make decisions. They simply follow their instincts and impulses. But before any person has been up three hours, he or she is compelled by the nature of existence to make decisions about life, about neighbors, about values. Christians are distinguished not by the fact that they live by faith but by the fact that they live by the faith that Jesus Christ is the revelation of God. In his light they seek to understand the common experiences of their lives. The church is the community in which people talk about life, its origin and its destiny, its meaning and its values, in the light of their common Christian conviction and under the norm of the Christian revelation.

Theology that is critical reflection upon the meaning of life and Christian theology that is reflection upon the meaning of existence in the light of God's presence in Jesus Christ is not undisciplined speech. It is not sharing personal opinions or making unsupported assertions. Theology is disciplined speech in a disciplined community. It is rooted in and loyal to the scriptures, which are the record of God's revelation. Theology is guided by the way in which Christians in all ages have understood that revelation. Theological discourse is, humanly speaking, the lifeblood of the church. Only as Christians engage in a common theological discourse can they embody the fullness of the church. Only in this way can the Christian community be distinguished from other communities, and only in this way can the Christian life be enriched, broadened, and deepened.

Evangelism is incorporation into a community of moral discourse. The Christian life is not following a party line; nor is it withdrawal from the political, social, or economic decisions of life. It is serious engagement with those issues in the light of faith commitments. The church is the place where the issues of the day can be analyzed, thought through, and acted upon in the light of the disclosure of God in Jesus Christ. The church is the community in which actual people are given real help in thinking through the real issues of their lives. It therefore has to be a community of moral discourse, as James Gustafson has said.[6] Again moral discourse is not undisciplined speech. It is not the sharing of personal opinions or unexamined convictions. It is disciplined discourse that is rooted in the Bible and the Christian tradition, and it takes place in the disciplined life of the Christian community.

Evangelism is incorporation into a community of worship. The one indispensable factor in the life of the church is the Word of God, and the high and central event in the life of the church is worship when the community gathers to hear the Word of God and to receive the sacraments, to adore, and to give thanks. Worship is the personal center of the community of theological discourse, of moral discourse, of mutual assistance and support. In worship, common life in a shared community is expressed in common prayer, hymns, and faith commitments.

Evangelism is incorporation into a community of being and action that embodies, however fragmentarily, the purposes of God for individuals and for the world. Karl Rahner, the Roman Catholic

6. Gustafson, *Church*, 84.

theologian, and Vatican Council II have rightly spoken of the church as the sacrament of the world.[7] It is the outward and visible sign, however broken, of the true reality of the world, and it exists to serve the world. The very existence of the church, as the sacrament of the world's true destiny, is a means of God's grace for the transformation of the world and for the healing of its wounds.

III

The great disparity between Calvin's Geneva and the last third of the twentieth century must be noted in any effort to relate evangelism and the Reformed faith. Between Calvin and twentieth-century Christians there stands the greatest break in all of humanity's intellectual and cultural history: the scientific revolution and the Enlightenment. There is a far greater difference between the way modern people think about the world and the way Calvin thought about the world than between Calvin and the disciples of Jesus. Furthermore, the relation of the church to society is radically different now from what it was in Calvin's Geneva or from what it was just a few years ago in our own history. We have passed from the parish church in Christendom (or in our own immediate past from the Protestant church in Protestantdom) to the voluntary church in a free, pluralistic, secular, mobile, urban, industrial society that is mass-media-dominated—or as Martin Marty summarizes, from a society in which all of the props of society support the church to a society in which few props support the church.

These two great changes are interrelated, and together they make the task of evangelism increasingly difficult. Less and less will society support specifically Christian styles of life. The church will have to become more and more responsible for its own life and for nurturing its own people, especially its young people and its married couples in the faith. In Calvin's words, "The church is the common mother of all the godly, which bears, nourishes, and

7. Rahner, *Church*, 18–19.

brings up children to God, kings and peasants alike; and this is done by the ministry."[8]

Evangelism can no longer assume that the masses know the meaning of the great Christian words or that society will support Christian faith commitments. For this reason evangelism is humanly dependent upon the renewal of the reality of the church.

IV

In classical Reformed theology, evangelism was not an identifiable, discrete activity of the church. It was the total life of the church. Today certain particular activities may be called evangelism for the sake of convenience, but for Reformed theology and ecclesiology any such activity must be integral to the whole life of the church. Evangelism is the church reaching out and incorporating those on the outside into its life.

The renewal of the church, humanly speaking—and by the same token, the renewal of evangelism—depends upon the theological competence and dedication of its ministers more than it does upon any other single factor. There is no possibility of any evangelism congruent with classical Reformed theology that is not supported and informed by a theologically competent minister and a theologically literate congregation. For this reason a great deal of the energy expended in seeking some new theology of evangelism or some modern technique of evangelism could more profitably have been used in basic Biblical and theological study. The same point must be made concerning studies of church management and the dynamics of groups. The church welcomes and uses all knowledge and techniques that are effective and agreeable to its convictions about God and man. But no mastery of group dynamics and process will ever make an evangelist out of a person who has not mastered the biblical material and who cannot or does not read serious theology.

8. Calvin, *Ephesians*, 282, on Ephesians 4:12.

Someone will protest that theology alone will not itself relate people to God or incorporate them into the church. This is true. Theology as an academic exercise or a parlor sport will not. But Calvin understood theology as a practical science, and he insisted that it must be understood and expressed in such a way as to illuminate life and to give meaning to common experience. Theology must speak of the grace of God in Jesus Christ in words that are intelligible. There is not as yet, nor is there ever likely to be, any substitute for the Christian, and particularly the minister, being a theologian.

Theology alone will not evangelize, for people must be engaged. Theology will evangelize only when it is confessed to actual people. In part this confession takes place through the life of the Christian community and its impact on the larger community. The early church made converts when those on the outside beheld in the church a life in which they wanted to share. Evangelism in this form continues to take place. Yet the church has always reached out through its members and invited those outside the life of the church to share in its common life. An old professor of pastoral theology used to say that a house-going preacher made a church-going people. The same is true in the wider context of evangelism. Calvin never faced this problem, for almost everyone in sixteenth-century Geneva was officially Christian. But it is likely to be increasingly our problem. For never in fifteen hundred years has there been so much freedom as now to be or not to be the church. As yet, no substitute has been found for individual Christians telling others about life and the grace they share in the church. Various forms of mass evangelism are supplements to, not substitutes for, personal evangelism in the context of the church.

V

Evangelism is the church's witness to the grace of God in Jesus Christ. No one has ever become a Christian apart from a witness who tells the story of God's love for that person in creation and redemption. Evangelism is the witness and the context in which a person comes to a knowledge of God in Jesus Christ—a knowledge that saves and transforms life. This knowledge of God's presence in Jesus Christ may come through years of gradual maturation in the church. It may come in a dramatic crisis that radically shifts the whole orientation of life. The work of evangelism is done when a person comes to confess that Jesus Christ is Savior and Lord.

God alone is the Savior. Neither the Christian community nor the witness saves except in a instrumental sense. No Christian tradition has emphasized this more than the Reformed. Yet this does not mean that human works are unimportant. Evangelism is the human works that have their warrant in the New Testament and that provide the ordinary occasion for human salvation.

Changes in our society make it critically important that the people who are the church must be very busy in the works of evangelism and Christian witness. For on the human level, the whole existence of the church is increasingly at risk in our society. Evangelism is telling a story. The stories that have shaped American life are now being challenged. On the secular level, chants on university campuses declare that Western civilization has got to go. The underlying assumption is that all cultures are equally good. In ecclesiastical and theological circles, pluralism is a new orthodoxy. The underlying assumption is not only that all forms of Christian faith are equally good, but that all religious stories have equal validity. The triumph of the Enlightenment is the notion that many roads lead to God.

Evangelism grows out of the conviction that in the providence of God, Jesus Christ is the Savior of the world, that on the cross he bore the sins of all people and that God raised him to be the Lord, not simply of the Christian community but of all human history. Evangelism is not just a church program or a technique but the passionate conviction that Jesus Christ is the Word made flesh for our salvation.

The church in recent years has had difficulty in saying that faith in Jesus Christ is *crucially* significant, not only for life on this planet but for human destiny. On the level of the church as the people of God, that is, the congregation, the issue is much clearer. *Apart from the passionate conviction that the story of the Bible culminating in Jesus Christ is my story and that God, in Christ, is my Savior, there is no convincing reason that a person should worship God in Christian churches or be the church at all.* Evangelism finally will become alive not through Assembly actions or bureaucratic pronouncements, but through the recovery of a passionate conviction.

VI

Evangelism, as shaped by the classical Reformed theology, is not a program nor a technique but the life of the church in its outreach and impact upon the world. Evangelism, understood in this way, should not be mistaken for the "old" evangelism, for the minister who is the preacher-teacher-theologian, even in a broken way, has been a rarity. Congregations that have been communities of theological and moral discourse and that have understood their existence as the embodiment of the purposes of God have been equally rare. Yet they do exist. Whenever such congregations have come into being, they have been the result of years of responsible churchmanship. *This churchmanship is the real program of evangelism.*

Evangelism, as the work and the life of the church in the world, does not mean that programs, techniques, or group skills are unimportant. Theology is certainly no substitute for visitation, for one person telling another person about the grace of God. Neither is theology a substitute for such mundane matters as records or prospect lists or systems for discovering the new people in a community. But all of these are subordinate to the theological and ethical life of the community, which on the human level validates everything else.

It must be said again, as the conclusion for this paper, that evangelism is the work of the spirit of God who speaks when and where he chooses and whose work can be neither programmed nor guaranteed. There is, however, the promise of God; and if we in the church do certain things, then it is more likely that the Church, which is the gift of God's grace, shall grow in our midst.

Bibliography

Barth, Karl. *Protestant Theology in the Nineteenth Century, Its Background and History*. Valley Forge, PA: Judson, 1973.

Calvin, John. *Commentaries on the Epistles of Paul to the Galatians and Ephesians*. Translated from the original Latin by William Pringle. Grand Rapids: Eerdmans, 1948.

Colwell, Ernest C[adman]. *New or Old? The Christian Struggle with Change and Tradition*. Philadelphia: Westminster, 1970.

Dawson, Christopher. *The Judgment of the Nations*. New York: Sheed and Ward, 1942.

Gustafson, James. *The Church as Moral Decision Maker*. Philadelphia: Pilgrim, 1970.

Hazelton, Roger. *New Accents in Contemporary Theology*. New York: Harper & Brothers, 1960.

Percy, Lord Eustace Percy. *John Knox*. London: Hodder and Stoughton, 1937.

Rahner, Karl. *The Church and the Sacraments*. New York: Herder and Herder, 1963.